ALSO BY PATRICK CHAPMAN

POETRY
Jazztown
The New Pornography
Breaking Hearts and Traffic Lights
A Shopping Mall on Mars
The Darwin Vampires
A Promiscuity of Spines: New and Selected Poems
Slow Clocks of Decay

FICTION
The Wow Signal
The Negative Cutter
So Long, Napoleon Solo
Anhedonia

the arts council / chomhairle / ealaíon
funding literature
artscouncil.ie

salmonpoetry

Publishing Irish & International

Poetry Since 1981

OPEN
SEASON
ON Patrick Chapman
THE
MOON

Published in 2019 by
Salmon Poetry
Cliffs of Moher, County Clare, Ireland
Website: www.salmonpoetry.com
Email: info@salmonpoetry.com

ISBN 978-1-912561-56-8

Cover photography and design: *Sean Hayes*
Typesetting: *Patrick Chapman & Siobhán Hutson*
Printed in Ireland by Sprint Print

Salmon Poetry gratefully acknowledges the support of
The Arts Council / An Chomhairle Ealaíon

Once again to Sara

Acknowledgements

Thanks to the editors of the following, where some of these poems first appeared, a few in earlier versions. 'Monkeymind', 'D. R. J.': *Poetry WTF?!*; 'The Portrait of a Lady as a Young Man', 'The Archivist': *The Cabinet of Heed*; 'Red Bush': *The Raintown Review*; 'Corpseflower', 'Torch, a Noun': *Visual Verse*; 'O', 'Stiletto and Fugue: Sonnets', 'In Heaven': *BlazeVOX*; 'Bulsara', 'Pilot': *Crannóg*; 'A Kindness': *The Stony Thursday Book*; 'A Model': *Anthology of New Roscommon Writing 2014–2018*; 'E', 'Vicky and Julian at Lafitte's': *SurVision* anthology; 'Beautiful Trick': *Smithereens*; 'Foreign Exchange': *Boyne Berries*; 'Finney, Welles & Co.': *Gargoyle*; 'An Orangewoman in New York': *Reading the Future*; 'American Dogs': *SurVision Magazine*; 'Tape Op', 'Wait for Me': *Flare*; 'Ophelia's Day Out': *The Irish Times*. 'D. R. J.' is a remix poem from a line of David Bowie's song, 'Starman'. 'Monkeymind' is a remix poem from many sources. 'O' was inspired by 19th-century advertisements for prophylactics, which I read in 1991, in *Blitz* issue 98. For their helpful reading of the work, my gratitude to the Peers, the Company of Words, Joanne Hayden, Maureen Gallagher and Dimitra Xidous. As ever, thanks to all at Salmon.

Contents

IV

V

VI

I

Jeez Louise

for D. K. L.

Thank you for your uterus. I keep it in a bell jar
on a shelf in the workshop. It's a beautiful thing,
an object of organic art no more unusual to me
than my routine of ordering the chocolate
shake in a silver goblet, and five or six
strong, sugar-charged coffees at the
same Naugahyde booth, in the
same Bob's Big Boy, at the
same time every day
for seven years.
I open my self.
The curtains
part. The
fish fly
in to
thrill
my
soul

and a woman in trouble stomps onstage. Jeez Louise, she
sings, just give the organ to someone who can use it —

so I tell her the uterus wants to be here
but she shuts me down with a finger

shaped like an eel to her lips
and reminds me that I am

a series of stills, not long
in projection. Three

reels, shown one
time only. Like

the producer who has
given me her womb

THANK YOU FOR YOUR UTERUS, RAFFAELLA

I too will lose the plot
device that introduces characters.

I smile and stir my
seventh cup of coffee.

The rabbits listen for the deer
to tell them where the owls have flown.

Here come the fish.

Here come the big

beautiful

mackerel of dreams.

A Model

To please a woman who will love it
you buy a perfect set of eight

human foetal skulls
at a Christchurch Market stall.

These crania, displayed
in drops of clear lucite,

you will fashion into an orrery
for her to wear

as a hat, her lovely
head, the sun.

This gift will correct
her impression of your

soul as a fragmented
concatenation

of nothings – within
each individual boundary

may be signs of industry
that no one has observed.

Now when you get
the objects home, you hear

her voice on the machine.
The solar system goes in the bin –

and twenty-five weeks
is Mercury —

twenty-seven weeks
is Venus —

twenty-nine weeks
is Earth —

thirty-one weeks
is Mars —

thirty-three weeks
is Saturn —

thirty-five weeks
is Jupiter —

thirty-seven weeks
is Uranus —

thirty-nine weeks
is Neptune —

Red Bush

I sip and read, read and sip. The hit
is just as they describe it on the box.
Refreshing, revitalising. Rooibos. The
plant itself is grown in the Cedarberg
region of the Western Cape. The blend
is naturally caffeine-free, which is good
to know. I've had my share of the jitters
today. It's low in tannin too — the copy
tells me — and it hydrates as efficiently
as water, a note designed to imbue me
with a general sense of wellness. Not
bad for a supermarket beverage. I set
the box on the table and put the cup
to my mouth. Indeed it does remind
me of something. I am not sure what
your man thinks he hopes to achieve
down there on his knees, tending
my garden, and me all settled on
the long divan, my stiff old pins
akimbo. Still, God loves a trier,
and as I sip this time, a wave
breaks softly on my lips.

Spotter

in   the   slow   time
              you   sit in
the   still   place
where   the
                    blood   falls
        one   drop then
                    one drop
                          and

        each one   waits
in   the   air
for   the   dying
          note
of   the   drop   before it
on   the   tiled floor where
through   the   cracks
  weeds   push up
              one   blade   then
        one
    blade
and   the   sun   when   it
          comes   sends nothing   at   all
          and

            the   day
                                        departs
in   a
        procession of
              seconds
that make   way   for
the   night
            and

              the   stars
        come out   unseen

17

O

Y u
need n t fear t
get a g   d supply f
these Letters, als kn wn
as Specialities, Pr tect rs,
Preventives &c. Made fr m
the finest Animal Skin r purest
Medicated and Vulcanised India-
rubber they are pr perly Cured
and Fitted with a steel c il Rim
thus can be r lled int a Spring
Pessarie and used as such by the
Wife. These instruments are
c nstructed in acc rdance with
the Female rganisati n. When
r lled int the n rmal shape they
can be w rn by the Husband and
effectively prevent Semen being
discharged int the Pr ductive
 rgans, making it imp ssible f r
anything t escape int the
Passage. N Apprehensi n need
be entertained f their g ing t
far. If cleansed and used acc rding
t instructi ns these Appliances may
be empl yed any number f times
ver a peri d f many M nths thus
pr viding a great c nvenience t
a pers n f limited means and will
be f und the m st reliable Articles
 f r this purp se. Available in
Circular r Cigarette F rm in three sizes:
N . 1: Small; N . 2: Medium; N . 3: Large.

The Old Pornography

for W. B.

Nin –

or dripping wax
on the nipples –

or velvet cuffs,   blindfolds,   beads,
gags,   straps,   an ice pop

to an orifice –   all as dull   as Flynt or Hef
and oh,   j'en ai marre,   P. Morrissey.

No – what you want
is a narcotic

and a labrador.
But wait.

What you need
is a programme of Boro

and one or more accomplices
to re-enact the films

from Goto,   Blanche   and Bathory
by way of   the Beast   and Miss Osbourne.

Forget   Emmanuelle   but don't
forget   the animation,   every cel.

To reproduce   that live   should sort
the pussies   from   the pricks.

II

Ophelia's Day Out

You'll smile to remember the emerald basque, velvet
on my freckled skin, and yes my Titian hair, bright
as we sit, a chaste pair, on a bank of the Dodder
with our ploughman's lunch and black beer.
Often troubled by simpleton princes,
I fear a disturbance in the bushes
but on our balmy afternoon
we have no such visitation —

and you'd hardly notice it —
as we try to catch our shadows
on the passing flits of minnows.
In a moment our tongues will meet
like lovers' tongues, as the river throws
a hissy fit.

The Portrait of a Lady as a Young Man

From a notebook found in the pocket of a 49-year-old woman, recovered following a trespass incident at 24th St. Mission Station, October 30th, 2017

The Particle Mule

Forty hours later I have showered twice
and still the musk of your body lingers
on mine, encoded in the fibres of
your green blouse. I have smuggled
traces of your scent across time zones
having cleansed my skin but carried
you with me, the organic Dior of you,
to America in your Banana Republic
pistachio shirt. I washed again
this morning then put on your avocado
chemise with the atoms of your ecstatic
come bound up in it; the dying aroma
of my own, degrading under yours.
I have brought you here to California
in your olive slipover and somehow
the border guards allowed you in.

The shortest day of the year. I wake in my hotel with a burnt lip and find myself out of cigarettes. I decide it is time to quit. And why stop with smokes? Why even get up? But at noon I go out to an exhibition on Brodsky, where my throat kicks in with a cough. My need blanks the letters yet here is the patronage of Akhmatova. Here is his arrest and trial for parasitism, for not earning enough to please the socialist authorities. Here, his time in the U. S. as Poet Laureate but no word of S. H. I must go to the store and buy more Camels. Who do I think I am looking for? The one I left at home? I force myself to focus. J. B. died at 55 of a heart attack, as I will likely do, if it is not emphysema or a train. Meanwhile I will soon attain the age of Kinsella's Christ with nothing to show but bruises and dependency — and who will there be to miss me when the moment comes? Everyone, of course. Everyone will miss it.

The Platonic Friend

Disappointed at the Hoover Pavilion
to find no vacuum cleaners, I get
hardly any sense of his turmoil, his life's

nothing. Then at the Cantor Center
I meet *The Kiss* again. I am blasted anew
by *Meditation* and *Three Shades* —

and it has been years since art
affected me. Today, although I am dead
I am also a thinker; and what is even

Brodsky beside one of these eternals? M
would know. M the philosopher,
who loved many kinds of music. M,

who welcomed me here a lifetime ago.
I thought then how tough it must be
to find yourself alone on campus

at Christmas far from home but no.
This was where M had time and space
in which to commune with her beautiful Aristocles.

Queen of the Nile

It seems calculated that you choose to live
on Love Lane, off Mount Street, and have

given me *Sexus* to bring on this trip as my
chaperone so that I might remember your

peach of an ass and not run off with someone
pointless. Miller's language is you to me now.

'Don't forget my porcelain peach of an ass,'
you'd said. 'Come back for it.' Instead

Sexus makes me think of your nipples,
hard as quantum mechanics to a cat;

and of your lips closing around my sleeping
cock to wake me up with a shock

the likes of which I have not had
since T the other year. Your pubic hair

feels manicured, or does it grow
that way in the wild, blue-black

and glistening, alive? Your Cleopatra bangs
stir in me a childhood pang for Taylor's

symmetrical face in Todd-AO, a crush
on television. Your southern accent —

soft as rain on difficult soil — infused with
a petrichor of intellect, inspires in your own

perpetually enraptured limbic system,
a river of delight, of wanton joy.

The Secret Guitarist

On El Camino Real, nothing is
    unreal. I will learn back in Dublin

that you have moved on to a part-
    time chamber musician in my

office. You meet him by chance
    then take him in hand for the mischief,

and everybody knows but I am too
    disturbed for them to risk breaking

the news. What if I crack? They fear
    that I might. Yet this is not for now.

Now in a Starbucks I hear a professor
    with her student discussing their love

like it is a research project
    that needs to be funded and will be

if certain impediments can be
    overcome. The professor chides

her young man. Is he not ill-mannered
    to go on with this affair

now that his wife is in chemo?
    But you in my mind are alive

and not here – and I would be no loss at all
    were you to slip me the Irish farewell.

The Barefoot Pandora

A mail from T pings in. *Who the fuck is N?*
    N is proof that Parker could be wrong.
Each love is not doomed

    to be the love before
but in a duller dress. As evidence, I offer
    your need to be a femme

fatale or to present yourself
    that way. It is endearing,
mostly to you, who so desire

    to be the one true Ava
Gardner. You call yourself a goddess
    of statues, a Pandora

Reynolds figure but you are not even
    Maria Vargas and I am not even
the wisp on the end of Bogart's stogie.

    By the time I get home to the fog
of the real, you will already be smoking
    someone else's Montecristo.

Palo Alto,
December 21st, 2000

29

Foreign Exchange

By the glass-bricked annex at Narodni,
a man trades us three thousand crowns

for a hundred dollars. 'Deal of the decade,'
he says. 'Deal of the year.'

In one of the new American bars, I call
for beers and find that he has given us

złotys. I pay with the last good currency
we have. Nothing to be done but drink

our Budvar, stare at the bottles and decide
there is no one to blame except Reagan,

maybe, or Gorbachev.
If the Wall hadn't fallen,

if the Yanks would only stay at home,
the city could remain bohemian.

We leave a tip of Polish paper
then take the map two miles

to our pensione, south of the TV tower
where this morning you defied vertigo.

'I am flying over Prague,'
you'd said, 'without wire.'

In my sleep the thief returns,
a golem forming from the plaster

in our Cabra walls. He squats in between us
as we watch Mr Blandings build a dream

house. You reach inside the creature's wrist
with your finger and thumb. You pinch

his clay vein open. Daylight beams out,
inscribing his new shem upon the dawn.

We rise and dress, famished
for breakfast served at a communal bench

as worksongs play. Black bread,
hard cheese, aged ham, boiled eggs,

and the gritty coffee I can taste
whenever I remember him —

that gone kid who matured
into this tired waste of meat.

Vicky and Julian at Lafitte's

In her teal bodice and Romantic tutu
Vicky works the till. She has scraped

her flaming hair into a bun that some
would call severe. Julian, débarrasseur,

swans in. He beseeches her to skip
this dive, elope with him. She sighs.

'I shall not marry any man,
for all I ever wanted was to dance.'

Vicky serves a customer then goes
to the cellar. She returns

with an armful of guns.
Water pistols, loaded. 'I have

hundreds in my armory,' she says,
then shoots, almost hitting Julian.

Her suitor falls away to brood.
She breaks the weapons out.

The patrons get busy, firing at will,
dodging spray, taking hits —

bodies thrown about the room
in a rite of apocalypse. What

a gun-happy lot, here in the old
pirate's Blacksmith Shop Bar, as

the mercury pushes a hundred and four
but the barmaid is cooler than anything.

Julian, struck by a stray drop – a tear
perhaps – from Vicky's gun, is flung

through a plate glass window. He spears
his torso on a shard. Technicolor blood

gushes to the floor, forming the outline
of two crimson pumps. The room falls

silent. Victoria's eyes become
starlost.

Gazing on Julian
buried in fragments,

the dancer remembers the last time,
when it was her.

The Grasse Spirit

your medium is
thread in forests

evergreen
raw silk strands

laced with menses
not always your own

flickering at midnight
ultraviolet on the structures

lunarbeams resolve
into a blueprint for your purity

reflection of Diana at your core
only last fall

did her namesake inspire
the weeping of nations

twist
a cosmic cat's-cradle

translucent co-ordinates
taut

between branches
pealing at the origin

geometry
of soul

The men at the bar had started to rant
about Arabs, so the four of us finished our
pastis, wrapped up our game of charades.
Outside, declaring open season on the moon,
you dared its face in a puddle to drown itself,
then dashed it with your bare feet. All the way
to La Rivolte we braved the rain until,
up at the villa, soaking in our clothes, we dive-
bombed the blue fluorescent pool. Lightning
flashed us whiter than white. I lost my grip
on the float and you took my arm. 'Hey,
Cousteau! Let me be your propeller.'

Drying out in bathrobes we sat about
the courtyard, smoking Gitanes untipped.
Jasmine, strong in my sinuses, tried to cuckoo
the tobacco — but darker fumes prevailed.
You talked of spirits, a stand you know
back home in Easthampton. One oak
in particular. When it was felled, the wood
nymphs refused to worry the stump. That tree
had quite the reputation. More than just a slut
for *Sciurus carolinensis*.

Now the smoke is a ghost
and our friends have retired. You muse
that apart from yourself, artists cannot swim
or drive. And ping-pong or boules? Forget it.
'Notoriously pitiful at ordinary life, artists
make terrible fathers.' That is why you'll never
sleep with one, especially not tonight. Yet isn't
fucking how the goddess keeps her abattoir supplied?
'Close,' you say, 'but no vagina.' Time to fly.

Fragrant from the evening, stepping dry
out of your robe you stand up willowy and nude
in moonlight — ultraviolet, statuesque.

Titania's Reflection

Spells

My Oberon has overdone it on
the Ambien. I think he'll rise in half
a cycle then, a sleepwalking giant,
raid the fridge. I've left a dish of Stilton
chilling on the rack for him; those blue-vein
dreams can be arousing. As I dress for
bed on this, an anniversary not
his, I watch him breathing and it is your
face I conjure, somewhere beyond the sea.
In a basement you pull out a box, to
find again a page from another life.
I remember that letter, green felt pen
on a paper bag wrapping my stories,
folded in a peach envelope, sealed with
a smack of pink lipstick. You pick it up
and can't decide if I had meant the kiss
for you, or as a passepartout for my
miniature fictions. You smile at the neat
hand in which I ask a reply with no
fonts, no setting, no style – for you had been
far too impressed by the clear acetate
on which I had sent an earlier note,
modern in Lucida Bright. You'd held that
one to the light, read it backwards for clues.
Do you keep this one now for a reason?
What compels you to come to the cellar,
seeking my voice in the dark? No matter.
My words, a midnight charm, return you to
a sudden morning twenty years ago.

Stars

We lie on my mother's lawn in summer,
a pair of grass angels watching the skies
like those kids in *Gregory's Girl*, except
we never say Caracas. Then we fill
a tipsy booth in Wylie's. You complain
of feeling stranded on the diving board
of life. I take your vodka stirrer, snap
the paddle, just like that. 'Jump in,' I say,
and you fall in love — not for the first time,
not for the last — with the impossible.

Shades

A decade again before this, I saw
no hint of mortal foolishness. You came
on a scholarship to my father's firm;
and I, the perfect host, took you to see
the latest Cronenberg. I admired but
did not love that dream of fruitful death. You
were wowed by Irons; struck by the languid
glamour of Bujold as Niveau; startled
at the sight of Heidi von Palleske, whose
open kimono exposed her auburn
beauty in the bathroom mirror as one
of the Mantle boys caught her reflection.
On leaving the screening you said, 'Cary
looks like you. She has your hair and face.' Now
what was I to do with that? So we hit
a yuppie bar halfway up a building
taller than you'd seen outside a movie.
Observing a business-wraith shooting up
in a corner, you felt mature, even
as you marked the coincidence of our
drinking Kronenbourg, calling it awesome.
At dinner that week, as *Blue Bell Knoll* played
overhead, the tricolore pasta
prompted you to ask if all glorious
things come in splendid colours. 'I sure do,'
I said, 'a lot.' Turning green, you excused
yourself for being jejune, a manchild
from a god-disfigured land that, ever
unconscious, never remembered to dream.

Signs

Do you get it now, old man? For all my
gifts I was no sybil. If I did not
foretell a day on Ponte Vecchio
when you, a donkey-head mechanical,
would purchase a pair of francobolli
to send me a card with no message, yet
assume that by the address I would know
who it was from – how was I to predict
the millennial month of our shared-brain
delirium, or my quick change of heart,
which floored you for years? How could I deny
my husband's name in giant letters – those
inexplicable graffiti – haunting
the old stone wall that waited in the park?
Did I not warn of the impossible?
We were broken going in – I, slipping
free of marriage to the wrong kind of ass;
you, having failed a woman beautiful
and true. That face in your wallet – her Jean
Seberg smile – I knew who it was had left
whom. Your heart was no more ready to beat
again than mine. So if you found in me
a meteorite that seemed to fit the
crater, I am blameless. Our rebounding
catastrophes repelled like opposing
magnets. I concluded honestly that
you were not the curative I needed.
Soon your kiss on my lips turned like milk left
out in a heatwave. I picked myself up,
then others. I piqued you with regular
breakdowns of every new fuck. You wanted
to know. You did. You seemed to need the eggs.

Strings

I've spent my life refining it, the art
of letting go of love. As a daughter
I learned it too well — how people remain
just as long as they will. Some are mayflies.
Others sustain you for a year or more.
Others still, hang on with a drowningman's
grip. The secret is to sense their time like
my dog can scent leukaemia, then to
detach with compassion. But it does not
always go that way. I imagine you
to lead a normal life with somebody
good — yet here you are, opening boxes.

Shards

I ask him, my Oberon du jour, if
a less distorted man than you, stepping
back from the ravine, would have missed the heights
of me. Or would he, mindful that my path
was never his, have taken it the same?
The sleeper has no answer. As for you,
it must be obvious by now how life
and memory diverge. When last we spoke
I said to have a blood test done — and if
it turned out clear, to bring it on a plane
across the ocean to my house. You would
come so that we could come. You did not come.
Tonight I hope you find my taste in your
mouth more curious and rich than bitter,
like the memory of a glorious
meal you once died for at a blue-ribbon
palace that closed many seasons ago.

                              Are you alive?

Shapes

Do you fold
    my old letters into origami boats composed of time,
      and call yourself profound?

Do you set
    our moments, every one, free upon the ebbing tide
      and think yourself exceptional?

Put it away,
    the porous flotilla. Forget
      the thrill of Ferry roaring *Prairie Rose*

as beneath your foggy window
    on the Irish sea, you licked wet salt from the come-
      taut skin of my supple, freckled belly.

Let him go,
    the man you were not meant to be. Jump in –
      and kindly never dream of me again.

III

Finney, Welles & Co.

When in heat, _____s will nest in heat. Last month in Grover's Mill, NJ, an area couple, making love, found their pillows infested by _____s, also making love. This was far from the kind of orgy the couple usually hosted in their home. Vigilance

is paramount, particularly in the desert, where cacti are Hilton Hotels for _____s. Hours after its arrival the *carnegia gigantia* a family practitioner in Mill Valley, CA, had shipped from a store, began to quiver in his kitchen like it was cold in there. It was

not cold. He phoned the army, who said put a bag on the specimen; your cactus is a Hilton for _____s. As he waited for soldiers to remove the shaking plant, the invasion was announced. From within the body of the cactus, burst a cluster bomb of baby _____s.

An Orangewoman in New York

Pour a glass of pekoe
   in your uptown brownstone — AC
busted, fan unturning,
   patchouli incense smouldering —

and consider the women
   of Little Phnom Penh, whose
autoblindness failed to quell
   the memory of napalm

seared into their vision.
   Western ophthalm-
ologists had passed their eyes
   as notblind, yet

the women had relinquished sight
   and gone to live in the OC.
I dare you to think ah well,
   as long as they got to say no.

Symbiont

Los Angeles, November, 2019

I had   the elements   of your life
dismantled,   cell   by   cell,

shipped over   into   mine
and   reappointed   in   a   smart

arrangement   designed
to answer   my   desire.

     It didn't take.

        Your   parts,

stripped   out of   their natural setting,   never fit
as   elegantly   as before   the   deconstruction.

So I had to admit   my   mistake. You've
got no utility,   I told you   as   gently

as   I   could. You are not required.
Go   and find a porch, I said. Go on,

find an old porch   to crawl under.
Don't wake me up   when you leave.

A Galaxy Craze Reader

The sun makes a shadow appear
more solid than the tree that sends it
on this fall Tuesday morning. An odd
couple rubs noses at the diamond. A priest
on a bicycle, swerves to miss a qi gong class
but keep her balance. A millennial baby
peers out from its father's elbow-cradle,
to burble at swans on the pond. I take

a bench to listen as a boy plays violin,
his back to a topless reader. Lotus
on a blanket she glances from her
novel, *By the Shore*, and smiles
across at me, her gaze framed
by the boy's bare legs.

Beautiful Trick

I temper the silence of these wretches
smoothly into mute admiration till
unholy raindrops scatter them and some
charge off to Café du Monde. Dirty pink
kevlar fanny packs bang on their crotches.
Only now I grab my porkpie hat – still
no rattle that might buy me a cool drink,
even a smoke. As you shelter I come

dancing in. My mouth shimmers the crimson
of the lamps that shine at night on Bourbon
latticework. I hear lovely thunder grow
louder as I snatch the wet cigarette
away from your cracked lips and make it glow
red in my hands, a star in a cornet.

The Zen Strangler

to kill is an act
of three perfect moves it takes
rare precision to

execute in one
instant the trained assassin
must break the windpipe

there is no second
attempt either the target
is ended or not

a killing has no
tenses no rhyme no season
the master moves like

lightning strike be gone
he cannot make a proper
kill if he is not

always prepared he
sits in his zen rockery
all day every day

meditating on
the moment his hands are so
attuned to even

the slightest flutter
of a cherry petal on
the breeze that his speed

is second nature
he renders all his targets
without consciousness

without consciousness
a true master exists on
the cusp of killing

when a target comes
the killer commands the act
and it is flawless

exemplifying
the ideal of perfection
the master lives by

Monkeymind

what   reality   star
pinocchio looks like now
is ridiculous hey sport
you are too fat to live
help me pinocchio youre
my only hope the chief
tells us this is how
mankind began you want
an easy and efficient way
out why hollywood wont
cast pinocchio anymore
shaping a hand from the
clay you must be fit and
healthy and attractive
i moved on pinocchio
like a bitch but I couldnt
get there you can not
live without all of those
delicious things the lord
of life took the hand and
pulled out a pink man
pale and weak too sad dc
area mother pinocchio
earns a billion a day
working from home you
are not doomed to be
gross and ugly for the
rest of your life the lord

turned the pink man
away ive gotta use some
tic tacs in case i start
kissing pinocchio if you
want a perfect solution
take my formula every
day the second man
brown the lord deemed
too strong one strange
tip to lose pinocchio in
just six days the lord
turned the brown man
away just wait for the
drugs to do the work
you got no need for
gyms and diets his third
creation pleased the
lord of life the trick
mr pinocchio is not
minding that it hurts
you will lose almost a
pound a day here try it
here for free here try it
his third creation was a
red man red like the
earth nobody pinocchio
not even the rain has
such small hands

Torch, a Noun

New York, 193–

the tunnel in your head
    that runs in all directions

                                           future
        passes through your face
                             past
        hits you from behind
                as it crashes into   future
        passes through your face
        as it

    each
        obliterates the other
            on contact

                too linear

    surely you would think

        it is a field
            unbound
                by dimension
            no present moment
                possible

    surely you are
        in the sense that
    you are

                neverending
    now

everywhere and always
as you occupy
all points

                                        as

                 the idea of time
                   loses gravity

                even as
                    a string of pearls

that Georgette may have
       worn if she had been

           everything to you

               and will be that
                   in a song

   you understand
      do you not
      understand

that every time is   now

               that nothing
rather than   everything

is what happens
       all at once

                       shut your eyes

consider

a man

tipping

his own

burnt skull

into

a well

consider

I

am

what

daisies

push

up

consider

chrononaut

agonistes

consider

someone has
cored   the apple

someone has stolen
the bowler

someone has peeled away the skin
and left only this

almost
copy

someone has left only this
someone has left only

someone has left
someone has

someone
some

so

s

∞

{∞}

{   }

}   {

you are

American Dogs

The   wiener   on   muscular
legs,   straining   at   your
leash,   stops   to   give   birth
by   the   metro   at   JZP.
A   crocodile
of   children   on   a   trip,
forms   into   a   scrum
that   eats   the   pups   then
eats   the   afterbirth.   You
let   go   of   your   empty   dog.
You   walk   the   mosaic-
panelled   stairway   to
the   trains,   which   run
on   time   through   dalek-
dimpled   tubes.   Mustek   waits
three   stops   along   and   out
on   Wenceslas   you   meet
your   tall   Angelena.

Half   an   hour   later   you   lie
with   her   in   the   flat
on   Dykova   while
in   the   other   room
Krappova,   your
German   landlady,
snores   like   a   file
as   she   dreams   of   bygone
springtime.   Beside   her
stands   a   drained   lemon
vodka   bottle   and   a   tray
of   extinguished   Petras.
Her   doberman   is   dead
on   a   dunghill   somewhere,
its   skull   split.
You   kiss   your   lover's   eyelids.
Then,   scissoring,
you   dream   the   new   breed.

Tape Op

The agent stalks the concrete floor. Stilettos it.
A lighter's click. A billowing of silk – then music.

You dance with her slowly as you smoke a Turkish
cigarette. The two of you fuck, a coupling of liars.

The song on the vintage cassette is the Beatles. *Let me
take you down*. She ties you to the chair. She folds

a satin cravat into your mouth. She seals the gap
with the kind of tape they use to mend linoleum.

I once read a story about a man who did himself in –
a hit of razor to the wrist. His wife was unimpressed

that he had bled on her linoleum. The agent slips
the needle in, a glass hypodermic, and you are done

with feeling. She cries above the plangent racket
of the Beatles' false

ending. I stop the tape. She listens for a moment to
my breathing – before calling the chauffeur and *let me*

take you down she leaves you undressed in the chair,
a frozen contortionist. I have seen nothing. I am

invisible. I don't give a damn. And as for you –
of course your name escapes me – what was lost,

exactly? Is not every human life in its entirety
a prelude to that instant of l'esprit d'escalier?

IV

The Hiss at the Birth of the Universe

constant
in   my
ears
as   if
some   engineer
recorded
all   of   reality
on   virgin
quarter
inch   and   I
am   hearing it
on   a   ferro
cassette
many   gene
rations   down
mastered
with   im
perfect
fidelity

Stiletto and Fugue: Sonnets

in here
with toys
and figurines
a few growlers
some are screamers
one a lycanthrope teddy
and pin is a boy who dreams
of becoming a real marionette
the asimo is addicted
to all kinds of cheese
he says addddicted
with a bad stutter
he says he is
emmental

big nurse shouts
here your tablets
eat and tomorrow
we try the red door
i can't wait i have to get
to the red door now which
of the toys will help me will
i die if i ask the copter because
in the red room
superior mother
waits to take me
home to the virgin
who runs the house
and has it in for copter

the asimo can't help me now
it is guzzling and pin the boy
who dreams of being wood
dreaming of being wood
cannot help me but
the ted is friendly
he says sure
he'll help
he drags me up in the air we
fly to the end of the ward
where he puts me down
and paddingtons away
he has to go morph
back into barbie

i crawl on the floor
until i reach the red
room and go thru
the red door and i see
no superior or virgin
where are they i see a
girl who looks like me
but is not me she is ten
x my size she is huge
she lifts my dress
she pulls on
my string
& i cry
mama
she
slit
me
here
mam
mama
she cut
me and
fucked
the red
wound
mama
mam
ma

In Utero

routine
        our nite
route in

                unite or
        untie or
                rein out

                roe unit
                        true ion
                outer in

                        one i rut
                                re in out
                        i rue not

Pilot

How did you persuade her to go with you? Was she
expensive? Was she good? You went for a stroll on the sea.
Why not use a boat? You admit you raised a corpse. You know
there's a law. You know it skews the market if you bring in the
undead. What was the deal with the fish and the loaves? How,
with slender means, did you produce those commodities in
such volume? Was that not a violation of quotas? You made
gallons of wine out of water. The military-industrial-
viticulture complex must have loved you for that. What do
you mean, you're a peacenik? Why destroy civic property
if you're so bent on being meek? Is your philosophy designed
to pacify the powerless? I see. Now this band of yours. Were
they your abductors? Your boyfriends? Why did they forsake
you? Why are your people so blind and so poor? Tell me how
you fool them into wanting only you. Why let our man kiss
you? Did you like it? You claim it was you who sent him; that
it wasn't his fault. Are you saying he is one of your lot? Should
we get our money back? I mean it. Should we? No – because
you *are* going to die. That's inevitable now. You are waiting
to die. You seem to *want* to die. Hold on – the kingdom of
where? Don't give me that. You are walking the via dolorosa,
my friend. It's no use looking at me. I don't care who you are.
I'd as soon let you go, if only –

What?

Fine.
I wash my hands.

    You are taking a plane to that tower
    and you're not coming back.

      That's all there is to it,
      my son.

Tönnchenform

Jesus Christ, tardigrade – the atmosphere
will kill you in a rush, no wait for slow

crucifixion. As the pressure rips your
flesh you won't feel your eyes evaporate.

Should you live through that, the radiation
guarantees a brutal death. The sudden

jump from furnace day to polar night is
fatal, so believe me, if you must go

you are sure to die of something: frostbite,
starvation, dehydration. Never leave.

Without you, how am I supposed to live?
Remember when the red sea parted us.

E

through   its   history   mercury
the   woman   in   black   lays   a   tablet

has contracted by a mile and a half in diameter
on your tongue and tells you to swallow

this makes you wonder what the effect has been
not chew and you must wait for her to begin

on property values there and if you should cancel
so   that   for   a   moment   you   feel   heaven

your   outing   to   the   beach   at   caloris
coming   in   at   both   ends

L

now   that   you   are   losing
skin   and   hair   and   sap

like   a   radiation   subject
sickened   by   the   shine

of   the   vital
shooting   past   you

with   their   fucking
and   enthusiastic   light,

carefree   as   a   particle
ignoring   the   screen

between   two   slits
then   coming   out   of   both

at   once,
it   is   time   you   screwed   it

to   your   head,
the   hat

at   the   drop   of   which
you   used   to   fall   in   love.

The Archivist

Yours is the last generation for whom
it will be possible to die of old age.

Your children and their offspring –
let's not trouble them with this.

I record my note for no posterity,
nor for the idea of posterity, which

we understand in terms of years
at best. Milton suddenly unspurred –

would he have persisted? That
is my task. I am putting

everything into the memory
vault so that whatever succeeds us,

though it be unfathomable,
and our artefacts invulnerable

to its comprehension, it will
see that something was here

before it. We, whatever
that might mean, were here.

Wait For Me

She whispers to her newborn
I will bring you up to hope –

for without hope, when you
meet the world as it is, your

sense of betrayal would not be
as acute, your disillusionment

not quite as refined – and if
to be alive is to be crushed,

why should you be different?
Who says you get off, scot-free?

In his mind the newborn answers:
come here and say that again

when more of me has emerged
into this, our blessed, sunlit earth.

Sehnsucht

The returned Apollo capsule
and the analogue landing module
in the foyer
recall Dallas as well
as Tranquillity. Together
with the Wrights' bird in the hall
they invoke
the name of Kitty Hawk. And there by the door,
under glass –
a moonrock,
a blister
on the lip of space –
unkissed five billion
years. To see it now, renews my sense
of isolation.
I am homesick for the incubator.

V

Contamination

<pre>
                    i
i   want
i   want   you
i   want   you   to
i   want   you   to   put
i   want   you   to   put   seed
i   want   you   to   put   seed   in
i   want   you   to   put   seed   in   me
it   does   not   have   to   be   your   seed
i   want   you   to   put   seed   in   me
i   want   you   to   put   seed   in
i   want   you   to   put   seed
i   want   you   to   put
i   want   you   to
i   want   you
i   want
                    i
i   want
i   want   him
i   want   him   to
i   want   him   to   put
i   want   him   to   put   seed
i   want   him   to   put   seed   in
i   want   him   to   put   seed   in   me
it   does   not   have   to   be   his   seed
i   want   him   to   put   seed   in   me
i   want   him   to   put   seed   in
i   want   him   to   put   seed
i   want   him   to   put
i   want   him   to
i   want   him
i   want
                    i
i   want
</pre>

```
i                   want                                her
i              want                      her              to
i          want              her              to          put
i       want          her          to          put        seed
i     want        her        to        put        seed      in
i   want      her      to      put      seed      in        me
it  does    not    have    to      be      her              seed
i   want      her      to      put      seed      in        me
i     want        her        to        put        seed      in
i       want          her          to          put          seed
i          want              her              to             put
i              want                      her                 to
i                   want                                     her
i                                                            want
                         i

i                                                           want
i                   want                                     it
i              want                      it                  to
i          want              it              to              put
i       want          it          to          put            seed
i     want        it        to        put        seed        in
i   want      it      to      put      seed      in          me
it  does    not    have    to      be      human            seed
i   want      it      to      put      seed      in          me
i     want        it        to        put        seed        in
i       want          it          to          put            seed
i          want              it              to              put
i              want                      it                  to
i                   want                                     it
i                                                            want
                         i

i                                                           want
i                   want                                   them
i              want                      them               to
i          want              them              to            put
i       want          them          to          put          seed
i     want        them        to        put        seed      in
```

78

```
i      want     them    to      put     seed    in      me
it     does     not     have    to      be      their   seed
i      want     them    to      put     seed    in      me
i        want     them      to        put       seed      in
i          want        them        to          put       seed
i            want          them          to        put
i              want          them                      to
i                    want                          them
i                                  want
                           i

i                                                  want
i                        want                      us
i              want                us              to
i          want          us          to          put
i        want        us        to        put      seed
i      want      us      to      put      seed      in
i      want      us      to      put      seed      in      me
it     does     not     have    to      be      our     seed
i      want      us      to      put     seed    in      me
i        want      us        to        put       seed      in
i          want        us          to          put       seed
i            want          us          to        put
i              want          us                      to
i                    want                          us
i                                                  want
                           i

i                                                  want
i                        want                      you
i              want                you             to
i          want          you          to          put
i        want        you        to        put      blood
i      want      you      to      put      blood      in
i      want      you      to      put     blood    in      me
it     does     not     have    to      be      your    blood
i      want      you      to      put     blood    in      me
i        want      you        to        put       blood      in
i          want        you          to          put       blood
```

79

```
i          want          you          to          put
i           want                you               to
i                   want                          you
i                                                 want
                    i

i                                                 want
i                    want                         him
i              want                   him          to
i          want              him          to       put
i       want          him          to     put    blood
i     want      him      to      put      blood     in
i     want     him     to     put     blood     in    me
it    does    not    have    to    be    his    blood
i     want     him     to     put     blood     in    me
i      want      him      to      put      blood    in
i        want           him           to         put
i              want                him            to
i                   want              him          to
i                        want                     him
i                                                 want
                    i

i                                                 want
i                    want                         her
i              want                   her          to
i          want              her          to       put
i       want          her          to     put    blood
i     want      her      to      put      blood     in
i     want     her     to     put     blood     in    me
it    does    not    have    to    be    her    blood
i     want     her     to     put     blood     in    me
i      want      her      to      put      blood    in
i        want           her           to         put
i              want                her            to
i                   want              her          to
i                        want                     her
i                                                 want
                    i
```

```
i                                                                    want
i                              want                                    it
i                     want                          it                 to
i                 want                    it                 to        put
i            want            it            to            put        blood
i          want        it        to        put        blood          in
i          want      it      to      put        blood      in        me
it      does    not    have    to      be      human        blood
i          want      it      to      put        blood      in        me
i            want        it        to        put        blood          in
i              want          it          to              put        blood
i                  want              it              to                put
i                      want                          it                 to
i                              want                                     it
i                                                                    want

                                   i

i                                                                    want
i                              want                                  them
i                     want                        them                 to
i                 want                  them              to          put
i            want          them          to          put          blood
i          want        them        to        put        blood          in
i          want      them      to      put        blood      in        me
it      does    not    have    to      be      their        blood
i          want      them      to      put        blood      in        me
i            want        them        to        put        blood          in
i              want          them          to            put          blood
i                  want            them                to                put
i                      want                      them                   to
i                              want                                    them
i                                                                    want

                                   i

i                                                                    want
i                              want                                    us
i                     want                          us                 to
i                 want                  us                to          put
i          want        us        to        put        blood
```

i   want   us   to   put   blood   in
i   want   us   to   put   blood   in   me
it   does   not   have   to   be   our   blood
i   want   us   to   put   blood   in   me
i   want   us   to   put   blood   in
i   want   us   to   put   blood
i   want   us   to   put
i   want   us   to
i   want   us
i   want

i

i   want
i   want   you
i   want   you   to
i   want   you   to   put
i   want   you   to   put   rage
i   want   you   to   put   rage   in
i   want   you   to   put   rage   in   me
it   does   not   have   to   be   your   rage
i   want   you   to   put   rage   in   me
i   want   you   to   put   rage   in
i   want   you   to   put   rage
i   want   you   to   put
i   want   you   to
i   want   you
i   want

i

i   want
i   want   him
i   want   him   to
i   want   him   to   put
i   want   him   to   put   rage
i   want   him   to   put   rage   in
i   want   him   to   put   rage   in   me
it   does   not   have   to   be   his   rage
i   want   him   to   put   rage   in   me
i   want   him   to   put   rage   in

i   want   him   to   put   rage

i   want   him   to   put

i   want   him   to

i   want   him

i   want

      i

i   want

i   want

i   want   her   to

i   want   her   to   put

i   want   her   to   put   rage

i   want   her   to   put   rage   in

i   want   her   to   put   rage   in   me

it   does   not   have   to   be   her   rage

i   want   her   to   put   rage   in   me

i   want   her   to   put   rage   in

i   want   her   to   put   rage

i   want   her   to   put

i   want   her   to

i   want   her

i   want

      i

i   want

i   want

i   want   it   to

i   want   it   to   put

i   want   it   to   put   rage

i   want   it   to   put   rage   in

i   want   it   to   put   rage   in   me

it   does   not   have   to   be   human   rage

i   want   it   to   put   rage   in   me

i   want   it   to   put   rage   in

i   want   it   to   put   rage

i   want   it   to   put

i   want   it   to

i   want   it

i   want

i   want

```
                        i
i                                                           want
i                       want                                them
i               want                    them                to
i          want              them               to          put
i        want          them          to          put        rage
i      want        them        to        put        rage    in
i    want      them      to      put      rage      in       me
it   does    not     have     to      be      their         rage
i    want      them      to      put      rage      in       me
i      want        them        to        put        rage    in
i        want          them          to          put        rage
i          want              them               to          put
i               want                    them                to
i                       want                                them
i                                                           want

                        i
i                                                           want
i                       want                                us
i               want                    us                  to
i          want              us                to           put
i        want          us          to          put          rage
i      want        us        to        put        rage      in
i    want      us      to      put      rage      in         me
it   does    not     have     to      be      our           rage
i    want      us      to      put      rage      in         me
i      want        us        to        put        rage      in
i        want          us                to          put    rage
i          want              us                to           put
i               want                    us                  to
i                       want                                us
i                                                           want

                        i
i                                                           want
i                       want                                you
i               want                    you                 to
i          want              you               to           put
```

i want you to put sick
i want you to put sick in
i want you to put sick in me
it does not have to be your sick
i want you to put sick in me
i want you to put sick in
i want you to put sick
i want you to put
i want you to
i want you
i want
i
i want
i want him
i want him to
i want him to put
i want him to put sick
i want him to put sick in
i want him to put sick in me
it does not have to be his sick
i want him to put sick in me
i want him to put sick in
i want him to put sick
i want him to put
i want him to
i want him
i want
i
i want
i want her
i want her to
i want her to put
i want her to put sick
i want her to put sick in
i want her to put sick in me
it does not have to be her sick
i want her to put sick in me

i want her to put sick in
i   want   her   to   put   sick
i   want   her   to   put
i   want   her   to
i   want   her
i   want

     i

i   want
i   want   it
i   want   it   to
i   want   it   to   put
i want it to put sick
i want it to put sick in
i want it to put sick in me
it does not have to be human sick
i want it to put sick in me
i want it to put sick in
i want it to put sick
i   want   it   to   put
i   want   it   to
i   want   it
i   want

     i

i   want
i   want   them
i   want   them   to
i   want   them   to   put
i want them to put sick
i want them to put sick in
i want them to put sick in me
it does not have to be their sick
i want them to put sick in me
i want them to put sick in
i want them to put sick
i   want   them   to   put
i   want   them   to
i   want   them

```
i                                                                    want
                          i
i                                                                    want
i                              want                                  us
i                      want                 us                       to
i               want            us                 to               put
i          want          us          to          put          sick
i        want        us        to        put        sick        in
i      want      us      to      put      sick      in       me
it     does     not     have     to      be      our      sick
i      want      us      to      put      sick      in       me
i        want        us        to        put        sick        in
i          want          us          to          put          sick
i               want            us                 to               put
i                      want                 us                       to
i                              want                                  us
i                                                                    want
                          i
i                                                                    want
i                              want                                  you
i                      want                 you                      to
i               want            you                to               put
i          want          you          to          put          come
i        want        you        to        put        come        in
i      want      you      to      put      come      in       me
it     does     not     have     to      be      your      come
i      want      you      to      put      come      in       me
i        want        you        to        put        come        in
i          want          you          to          put          come
i               want            you                to               put
i                      want                 you                      to
i                              want                                  you
i                                                                    want
                          i
i                                                                    want
i                              want                                  him
i               want                       him                      to
```

87

i　　　want　　　him　　　　to　　　　put

i　　want　　him　　　to　　　put　　come

i　　want　　him　　to　　put　　come　　in

i　　want　　him　　to　　put　　come　　in　　me

it　　does　　not　　have　　to　　be　　his　　come

i　　want　　him　　to　　put　　come　　in　　me

i　　want　　him　　　to　　put　　come　　in

i　　want　　him　　　to　　　put　　come

i　　want　　him　　　　to　　　　put

i　　want　　him　　　　to

i　　　want　　　him

i

i　　　　　　　　　　want

i

i　　　　　　　　　　　　　want

i　　　　　　want

i　　want　　her　　　to

i　　want　　her　　to　　put

i　　want　　her　　to　　put　　come

i　　want　　her　　to　　put　　come　　in

i　　want　　her　　to　　put　　come　　in　　me

it　　does　　not　　have　　to　　be　　her　　come

i　　want　　her　　to　　put　　come　　in　　me

i　　want　　her　　to　　put　　come　　in

i　　want　　her　　to　　put　　come

i　　want　　her　　to　　put

i　　want　　her　　　her　　to

i　　want　　her

i

i

i　　　　　　want

i　　want　　it

i　　want　　it　　to

i　　want　　it　　to　　put

i　　want　　it　　to　　put　　come

i　　want　　it　　to　　put　　come　　in

i　　want　　it　　to　　put　　come　　in　　me

it　　does　　not　　have　　to　　be　　human　　come

```
i      want      it      to      put      come      in      me
i      want      it      to      put      come      in
i      want      it      to      put      come
i      want      it      to      put
i      want      it      to
i      want      it
i      want

                    i

i                                                          want
i                          want                            them
i                  want                    them            to
i              want              them              to      put
i          want          them      to      put            come
i        want        them      to      put      come      in
i      want      them      to      put      come      in      me
it      does      not      have      to      be      their      come
i      want      them      to      put      come      in      me
i        want        them      to      put      come      in
i          want          them      to      put            come
i              want              them              to      put
i                  want                    them            to
i                          want                            them
i                                                          want

                    i

i                                                          want
i                          want                            us
i                  want                    us              to
i              want              us                to      put
i          want          us        to      put            come
i        want        us        to      put      come      in
i      want      us      to      put      come      in      me
it      does      not      have      to      be      our      come
i      want      us      to      put      come      in      me
i        want        us        to      put      come      in
i          want          us        to      put            come
i              want              us                to      put
i                  want                    us              to
```

89

```
i                 want                                        us
i                 want                                        want
                            i
i                                                             want
i                    want                          you        you
i                 want              you                 to     to
i              want          you          to       put        put
i            want      you       to    put     joy            joy
i          want     you     to   put    joy    in             in
i        want    you    to  put   joy   in   me               me
it       does   not  have  to   be   your   joy               joy
i        want    you    to  put   joy   in   me               me
i          want     you     to   put    joy    in             in
i            want      you       to    put     joy            joy
i              want          you          to       put        put
i                 want              you                 to     to
i                    want                          you        you
i                                                             want
                            i
i                                                             want
i                    want                          him        him
i                 want              him                 to     to
i              want          him          to       put        put
i            want      him       to    put     joy            joy
i          want     him     to   put    joy    in             in
i        want    him    to  put   joy   in   me               me
it       does   not  have  to   be   his    joy               joy
i        want    him    to  put   joy   in   me               me
i          want     him     to   put    joy    in             in
i            want      him       to    put     joy            joy
i              want          him          to       put        put
i                 want              him                 to     to
i                    want                          him        him
i                                                             want
                            i
i                                                             want
i                    want                                     her
```

90

```
i            want               her                      to
i         want            her            to              put
i       want          her          to          put       joy
i      want       her      to      put      joy          in
i     want     her     to     put     joy     in        me
it    does    not     have    to     be      her        joy
i     want     her     to     put     joy     in        me
i      want       her      to       put      joy         in
i       want          her          to          put       joy
i         want            her            to              put
i           want                her                      to
i                 want                                    her
i                                                        want

                          i

i                                                        want
i                 want                                    it
i            want                it                       to
i         want            it            to               put
i       want          it          to          put        joy
i      want       it      to      put      joy            in
i     want     it     to     put     joy     in          me
it    does    not     have    to     be     human        joy
i     want     it     to     put     joy     in          me
i      want       it      to       put      joy           in
i        want         it          to          put         joy
i          want            it              to            put
i                 want                it                  to
i                        want                             it
i                                                        want

                          i

i                                                        want
i                 want                                   them
i            want                them                     to
i         want            them            to             put
i       want          them          to          put      joy
i      want       them      to      put      joy          in
i     want     them     to     put     joy     in        me
```

it   does   not   have   to   be   their   joy
i   want   them   to   put   joy   in   me
i   want   them   to   put   joy   in
i   want   them   to   put   joy
i   want   them   to   put
i   want   them   to
i   want   them
i   want
i

i   want
i   want   us
i   want   us   to
i   want   us   to   put
i   want   us   to   put   joy
i   want   us   to   put   joy   in
i   want   us   to   put   joy   in   me
it   does   not   have   to   be   our   joy
i   want   us   to   put   joy   in   me
i   want   us   to   put   joy   in
i   want   us   to   put   joy
i   want   us   to   put
i   want   us   to
i   want   us
i   want
i

i want you to put
your next miscarriage in me

VI

Blvd

for J. G. B.

i n t h i s e v

a p o r a t e d

s w i m m i n g

p o o l a b a n

d o n e d b y t

h e f i l m a c

t r e s s t h e

t e r r a z o g

r i d i s v e i

n e d w i t h v

a r i c o s e l

i a n a s a s a

b o v e i t a c

e s s n a d i v

i d e s t h e s

k y i n a t e m

p o r a l e c h

o o f a d i v e

Demon Days: Dance Phase [08]

[what facility your hands slip around my neck as
if to measure me for morning wear] I am no longer

listed as single. [with   facility your hands slip
around my neck as if to measure me for morning wear]

I have had an almond croissant. I promise to call it.
[with what   your hands slip around my neck

as if to measure me for morning wear] I love the new
Forster-McLennan   song. [with what   facility

hands slip around my neck as if to measure me for
morning wear] I prefer the freshly dead Owen Harper.

[with what facility your   slip around my neck as
if to measure me for morning wear] I am making little

mind babies and putting them out on the conceptual
mountaintop to see which ones survive the night. [with

what facility your hands   around my neck as if to
measure me for morning wear] I am biodegradable,

mostly. [with what facility your hands slip   my
neck as if to measure me for morning wear] I am tired

of life but not, curiously enough, of London. [with
what facility your hands slip around   neck as if to

measure me for morning wear] I am now minus twelve
on the Richter scale. [with what facility your hands slip

around my   as if to measure me for morning wear]
I am isomorphic, except on Thursdays. [with   what

facility your hands slip around my neck   if to measure
me for morning wear] I am using factor 50 to protect

against the eternal sunshine of the spotless mind. [with
what facility your hands slip around my neck as   to

measure me for morning wear] I am no longer listed as
in a relationship. [with what facility your hands slip

around my neck as if   measure me for morning wear]
I mostly write at night, mostly. [with what facility your

hands slip around my neck as if to   me for
morning wear] Give me phenobarbital and Belvedere,

or give me death. [with what facility your hands slip
around my neck as if to measure   for morning wear]

I have no charm against these last five days. [with what
facility your hands slip around my neck as if to measure

me   morning wear] My joie de vivre is wearing out. [with
what   facility   your   hands   slip   around   my

neck as if to measure me for   wear] 'Could you be
more ... specific?' [with what facility your hands slip

around   my   neck   as   if   to   measure   me   for
morning   ] Nothing important happened today.

Quite Useless

no   the point is
no one   reads it
until after   you are dead

if you meant   to cry for help
why did you   write it
as a song   when of the few

who noticed   fewer
listened   and of those
fewer   heard

most are apt   to think it is
your creatures   not you
who are in   trouble

and how   impolite you are
for inventing   idiots so vile
did you not intend   that the listener

would never   understand
and how should you   expect
them to   understand

that it is you   caged in such a brain
the very lines   your jail
you always hide   behind the bars

now take up   your blade
go write   your note again
and this time mean it   this time do it right

Bulsara

Powerless to pirouette,
  you were helped to the limousine

that carried you to Harley Street back doors,
  eluding the jackals who called you gaunt.

Having all the 'fuck you' money
  in the world, you blessed your dears with homes —

and how your spirit must have smiled in the booth
  as you laid down your vocals to finish the band.

These days you appear
  where your ghost light never dims —

to whisper a cappella arias
  in brokenhearted boudoirs.

Boulder of Smoke

Where does it come   the break
  At what point
    does a life become

                only a past

a stone

             to push up a hill that has
       no peak   A stone that never
      rolls back down   [No Sisyphus

         who rested]
When   did it descend   the brume
  in which   you have moved
    for you cannot   remember   how long
     Who can say   for how long
     within it   you may persist

Half-life

My   notghost
    on   a   neverday
do you read me
    In the year of twenty twenty two
are you as old
    as   I   was   when
[No
    You   are

not]   You   never
had   a   beat
to measure   time
    and   give   your
        mortal   universe
        duration

A Kindness

slumped in a seat on a train
                              stitching the hem of a moiré
sea
          bound for it won't matter where
                              you glance
up at a hand strap
                              pendulous purple vinyl loop
on a yellow steel rail
                              and curse your daft old head
for being too fat to go through

                    oh if it could
you might hang there for days
                              before anyone thought
to look up from his tablet

                    [

                    now that you live
entirely within
                    the pale of another
country

now that your earlier
                              selves
are beyond it

                              you have nothing
to call your own

                    ]

no you will not use the strap
                              it reminds you of a woman's weeping

                    instead you may stumble
out at a station and wait
                    or walk a little way
find a spot to wade in
                    say
                    the rockfall that deformed
the beach
                    when victorians gouged the earth

                                        yes you

could go in there

                    dash your skull on a grey stone

yes

    you could lie adrift awhile

                    paling in the rain

The Failure

my tiny knife surprises   with its bite
    i draw the blade

    hard across the back   of my bare arm
just above the wrist   the hairs stand up

i breathe in sharply   i was not   expecting
    this   the blood line pulses out

& runs
towards my knuckles   quick

i pull the knife   wipe   it on
my trouser thigh   i turn

    the hand   a crippled tarantula   legs
jutting in the air   the cloth

absorbing the blood &   you see none of this
    but keep on

eating   i
excuse myself   i need to

go   i say   my bladder crying
    out

& in

　　　your bathroom
on the porcelain　　　　　　　　the blood looks brown

in tapwater flow　　　　it stirs　　　a memory
　　　of meat　　　when i was　　　　a girl

　　　look here　　the slabs　　　on stainless steel
in violet light　　grey steaks

the flies
roamed freely then　　　　& no one

　　　thought to lie

before i go downstairs

　　　　　　　　　　　i change
into my long-sleeved　blue silk blouse

just
　　　　　　　dark enough

Cruise's Vein

A surgeon
     slices your   testicle
and reveals in
     the meat   a human
  molar   crumbling,
    leaving   a residue
      of blue   powder
     in the   wound.

               Is this death?

     At first   the dream
      makes you fear
       it might be so.

Checking turns
      compulsive.
The semen
      appears   alternately
   diluted and
     coagulated.

     The nurse
      as he   rubs
   the green   gel in
      for the scan,
  laughs and   says relax,
   I'm not
    a queer.

Your doctor
            gives   the all-clear
but no answer
                  only   put it
      out of your mind.

So you   conjure
      undetected   metastasis.
                        Do you have
            the virus   or is it

            the C-   word?

A second   doctor
                tells you
        that your   problem

                  is a figment   made
      elaborate.
                She says
      man up
                        and get   a life.

                  But
six days on,
                you jump

      off the   Vincent
                Thomas   Bridge
            and leave

                  no
                        note.

Suspender

I enter the wound   in your side
with my fist   I open   my fingers

                    You weep

great drops   of sputum   and blood

    I pull your
       heart out

    snag my wrist
       on a rib stump

      blood flows
    down across my lifeline

Your   organ   implodes
pyramid   auricles   ventricles

            do this in
                 memory

      Two
   irises form on the sun

  and as those eyes bleed
yours close

        and the body
           dissolves

     with a raincloud
         crack

   and nothing remains
         but a story

Scarecrow

            look at   you

   up   on that   hill

  addressing   half   a crowd

                  of   half-believers

 just   look

   at you

posing

for   the   statues

we   will   not be   pulling down

even   after the   millions whom

  your   gentle

    sacred   scarecrow

      words   will   kill

Surrender

there are no years

nobody knows

how time is reckoned

it goes unrecorded

how many we are

kneeling in the square

before a dais that reaches

from here to eternity

as we praise the leader

for how long none can say

and it does not

feel like forever

as the leader observes

the infinite parade

of interdimensional

ballistic lightning bolts

passing on the backs

of military unicorns

Corpseflower

February 1st, 2018

You turn up dead again, old friend,   having
drawn the sky down to wear blue like   a veil
composed of gas, your cold meat   insisting
on a few hours more of seeming   alive
with no sign of decomposition —   yet
who, in a week, will say that you were   here
let alone what volume you displaced?   For
a whole world must go on and you must   not

see it, hear it, touch it, taste it, smell it.   Please
tell, if you can, what senses you are   missing
now, that you did not know you had. Too   late
you breathe your veil in deep then expel   it
shallowing. All inspiration may   cease
but won't. Only yours. Only now.   Nothing.

In Heaven

           eat
                sleep

I   piss

                            drink

when it is time for us to   fuck

                wake

           shit

                all day the kindly angel watches over us

                  we must ever love the angel or be lost

every night I press the pillow to my face

it never works

                      every day   I

                   wake and   cry

           to   kill

        the   scream   not

   this   again

   not   this

D. R. J.

Manhattan, January 10th, 2016

L	R
the wireless had	the wireless had
to tell someone	to tell someone
so it picked on	so it picked on
me the	me the
wireless had to	wireless had to
tell someone	tell someone
so it	so it
picked on me	picked on me
the wireless	the wireless
had to	had to
tell	tell
someone so it	someone so it
picked on me	picked on me
the	the
wireless	wireless
had	had
to	to
tell	tell
someone	someone
so	so
it	it
picked	picked
on	on
me	me
on	on

picked   picked
it   it
so   so
someone   someone
tell   tell
to   to
had   had
wireless   wireless
the   the

picked on me   picked on me
someone so it   someone so it
tell   tell
had to   had to
the wireless   the wireless

picked on me   picked on me
so it   so it
tell someone   tell someone
wireless had to   wireless had to
me the   me the
so it picked on   so it picked on
to tell someone   to tell someone

the wireless had   the wireless had

to tell someone   to tell someone
so it picked on   so it picked on
me the   me the
wireless had to   wireless had to
tell someone   tell someone
so it   so it
picked on me   picked on me

the wireless   the wireless
had to   had to
tell   tell

someone so it   someone so it
picked on me   picked on me

the   the
wireless   wireless
had   had
to   to
tell   tell
someone   someone
so   so
it   it
picked   picked
on   on

me   me

on   on
picked   picked
it   it
so   so
someone   someone
tell   tell
to   to
had   had
wireless   wireless
the   the

picked on me   picked on me
someone so it   someone so it
tell   tell
had to   had to
the wireless   the wireless

picked on me   picked on me
so it   so it
tell someone   tell someone
wireless had to   wireless had to

me the me the
so it picked on so it picked on
to tell someone to tell someone

the wireless had the wireless had
to tell someone to tell someone
so it picked on so it picked on
me the me the
wireless had to wireless had to
tell someone tell someone
so it so it
picked on me picked on me

the wireless the wireless
had to had to
tell tell
someone so it someone so it
picked on me picked on me

the the
wireless wireless
had had
to to
tell tell
someone someone
so so
it it
picked picked
on on

me me

on on
picked picked
it it
so so
someone someone

tell tell
to to
had had
wireless wireless
the the

picked on me picked on me
someone so it someone so it
tell tell
had to had to
the wireless the wireless

picked on me picked on me
so it so it
tell someone tell someone
wireless had to wireless had to
me the me the
so it picked on so it picked on
to tell someone to tell someone

the wireless had the wireless had

to tell someone to tell someone
so it picked on so it picked on
me the me the
wireless had to wireless had to
tell someone tell someone
so it so it
picked on me picked on me

the wireless the wireless
had to had to
tell tell
someone so it someone so it
picked on me picked on me

the the

wireless wireless
had had
to to
tell tell
someone someone
so so
it it
picked picked
on on

me me

on on
picked picked
it it
so so
someone someone
tell tell
to to
had had
wireless wireless
the the

picked on me picked on me
someone so it someone so it
tell tell
had to had to
the wireless the wireless

picked on me picked on me
so it so it
tell someone tell someone
wireless had to wireless had to
me the me the
so it picked on so it picked on
to tell someone to tell someone

the wireless had
to tell someone
so it picked on
me the
wireless had to
tell someone
so it
picked on me

the wireless
had to
tell
someone so it
picked on me

the
wireless
had
to
tell
someone
so
it
picked
on

me

on
picked
it
so
someone
tell
to
had
wireless

the wireless had
to tell someone
so it picked on
me the
wireless had to
tell someone
so it
picked on me

the wireless
had to
tell
someone so it
picked on me

the
wireless
had
to
tell
someone
so
it
picked
on

me

on
picked
it
so
someone
tell
to
had
wireless

the	the
picked on me	picked on me
someone so it	someone so it
tell	tell
had to	had to
the wireless	the wireless
picked on me	picked on me
so it	so it
tell someone	tell someone
wireless had to	wireless had to
me the	me the
so it picked on	so it picked on
to tell someone	to tell someone
the wireless had	the wireless had
to tell someone	to tell someone
so it picked on	so it picked on
me the	me the
wireless had to	wireless had to
tell someone	tell someone
so it	so it
picked on me	picked on me
the wireless	the wireless
had to	had to
tell	tell
someone so it	someone so it
picked on me	picked on me
the	the
wireless	wireless
had	had
to	to
tell	tell
someone	someone

so   so
it   it
picked   picked
on   on

me   me
on   on
picked   picked
it   it
so   so
someone   someone
tell   tell
to   to
had   had
wireless   wireless
the   the

picked on me   picked on me
someone so it   someone so it
tell   tell
had to   had to
the wireless   the wireless

picked on me   picked on me
so it   so it
tell someone   tell someone
wireless had to   wireless had to
me the   me the
so it picked on   so it picked on
to tell someone   to tell someone

the wireless had   the wireless had

to tell someone   to tell someone
so it picked on   so it picked on
me the   me the
wireless had to   wireless had to

tell someone   tell someone
so it   so it
picked on me   picked on me

the wireless   the wireless
had to   had to
tell   tell
someone so it   someone so it
picked on me   picked on me
the   the
wireless   wireless
had   had
to   to
tell   tell
someone   someone
so   so
it   it
picked   picked
on   on

me   me

on   on
picked   picked
it   it
so   so
someone   someone
tell   tell
to   to
had   had
wireless   wireless
the   the

picked on me   picked on me
someone so it   someone so it
tell   tell
had to   had to

the wireless
picked on me
so it
tell someone
wireless had to
me the
so it picked on
to tell someone

the wireless had

to tell someone
so it picked on
me the
wireless had to
tell someone
so it
picked on me

the wireless
had to
tell
someone so it
picked on me

the
wireless
had
to
tell
someone
so
it
picked
on

me

the wireless
picked on me
so it
tell someone
wireless had to
me the
so it picked on
to tell someone

the wireless had

to tell someone
so it picked on
me the
wireless had to
tell someone
so it
picked on me

the wireless
had to
tell
someone so it
picked on me

the
wireless
had
to
tell
someone
so
it
picked
on

me

PATRICK CHAPMAN has published eight poetry collections since 1991, as well as a novel and three volumes of stories. His other works include a short film, television for children, and audio dramas for *Doctor Who* and *Dan Dare*. He produced B7's dramatisation of Ray Bradbury's *The Martian Chronicles* for BBC Radio 4. With Dimitra Xidous he edits *The Pickled Body*.